CW01309654

Meet Me by the Monkey Bars

Helena Denton

AuthorHouse™ UK Ltd.
500 Avebury Boulevard
Central Milton Keynes, MK9 2BE
www.authorhouse.co.uk
Phone: 08001974150

©2007 Helena Denton. All rights reserved.

No part of this book may be reproduced, stored in a retrieval system, or transmitted by any means without the written permission of the author.

First published by AuthorHouse 8/30/2007

ISBN: 978-1-4343-2271-5 (sc)

Printed in the United States of America
Bloomington, Indiana

This book is printed on acid-free paper.

This book is dedicated to my sisters Sue and Sheila, who made my childhood great fun. Without them life would not have been an adventure.

This story is about having fun, and using our imagination. Those were the days of making dens, and climbing trees. We would be outside playing, from the morning right through to bedtime. It was the time before computer games and children muttering, "I am bored!"

This is my story through the eyes of a child.

My love to my husband John, and my two special children: Craig and Natalie.

Chapter One

I was born on the 10th July 1964, on the channel island of Jersey. My name is Maria Helena Costa; I was always known as Helena. My parents are called Leonel and Aldina. They are Portuguese and had come from the hot island of Madeira, to Jersey, to look for work.

There are five in my family: mum and dad, two sisters, and me. My family have all black hair, brown eyes and olive Mediterranean skin, however that is where the similarities end.

Dad was very tall. He always smelt of a mixture of boiled sweets and cigarettes, as he was trying hard to give up cigarettes. Everyone thought he was the kindest and funniest person. This was true, if you weren't a family member.

Helena Denton

With our family he had strange moods. On some days he would be the happiest person, and give you his last penny. Then suddenly he would become grumpy and very argumentative, and nothing could change his mood. My sisters and I soon learned to recognise these mood swings, and would know how the day would turn out.

Mum was much smaller than my dad. She always dressed smartly and never went out of the house without a clean hanky in her handbag. Mum spoke better English than my dad; everyone knew she was the wise one.

They were very strict and would stand no nonsense, and woe betide anyone who disobeyed them. We girls would often feel the slipper across our backsides, if our behaviour wasn't up to scratch.

I have two sisters. Susan was the oldest, very arty and very clever. Then there was Sheila, the youngest, the daring one — always up for a challenge. I was the middle one. Mum and dad would always say, "Listen to Sue, she's the oldest," or "Sheila's only little, let her have it," in response to whatever we were quarrelling about. Middle ones are never treated fairly; it was never my turn.

My story begins at 64 Troy Court. We lived in a block of flats four stories high. Our flat was on the top floor, after climbing the 80 steps, 20 on each floor. When the front door opened it led straight into the living room. This was large sunny room,

Meet Me by the Monkey Bars

with very large horrible bright yellow flowered wallpaper. It had loads of photographs of all the family. However much to my embarrassment the first photographs anyone saw when coming to our home were three huge photographs which hung on the main wall, showing us girls as babies, with no clothes on.

On the other wall was a Portuguese plate, next to it was a British plate with the Queen on it. Mum loved the fact that she and dad were Portuguese. Now they felt very British too.

We had a small kitchen that always had a huge basket filled with courgettes, onions, and goodness knows how many other vegetables. Mum and dad always thought this was the most important part of the house. Nobody left our house without having something to eat, otherwise my parents would have felt this was an insult to them.

There were three bedrooms. Mum and dad's had a huge picture of the Pope above their bed. Mum had a dressing table, full of little ornaments which we had bought her each birthday. The other table was dad's, this was filled with football magazines, which he cut up and then stuck on large card; sometimes he would stick them on their bedroom wall. Mum would say, "Not next to the Pope," and dad would reply, "You think he doesn't like football too?" Mum would always shake her head in disgust. Mum was really happy when I brought a scrapbook home from school and told dad to stick the pictures

Helena Denton

in this book. "That's what the English people do," I told him. He was happy then, and would spend many hours sticking cuttings in this book.

Sue's bedroom was the best room in the house. She had pink wallpaper. The room had a large window, which always made it look really bright. In her room was a matching wardrobe and dressing table with a small pink seat. Sue always kept everything tidy; all her books were stacked neatly on shelves. She had a small table with all her art pencils and coloured paper, and even a small pot of assorted paperclips. It looked very grand and I was very jealous. Her room was covered in Bay City Rollers' posters, and a tartan scarf hung above her bed.

My bedroom was shared with Sheila. It was a small pokey room, with two single beds and a horrible old black wardrobe, which dad had been given by someone. My side of the room was covered in Donny Osmond posters, however Donny suddenly appeared to have been given a moustache, by one of my sisters, which one I don't know, but I have my suspicions. On my bed there was my beloved teddy, a grey elephant, a pink cat, a blue rabbit with one ear, and a smiley Golliwog. I loved these cuddly toys and would try and sleep with them all; I was always squashed, but I couldn't bear for them to be cold. I had a large poster of Manchester United, because I thought the goalkeeper was cute.

Sheila's side was filled with plastic animals — not the cute kind, but spiders and scorpions. She had a large poster of a snake eating a mouse, which was disgusting, which I hated the look of. But I loved sharing my room with Sheila, as I loved to chat constantly, much to Sheila's annoyance— who would threaten to beat my teddy up, if I didn't shut up and let her go to sleep.

I loved Troy Court; it seemed very big to an eight-year-old. There were several large grassy areas and a stream that ran the length of the estate. The best part of the estate was the woods at the back of the flats.

The estate just seemed to have everything, especially a huge muddy grass bank and loads of trees and places to hide. There was a huge rope for a swing on a large old tree, and places galore to make home-made camps. Us kids loved to play outside. There was always an abundance of children around and always someone to play with.

Each flat had a garage; ours was number 4. Because my dad worked long hours in a hotel our garage was a good place to play. It was great because dad had collected loads of rubbish but couldn't bear to throw anything away. So all this junk made brilliant camps, and us children would spend many happy hours entertaining ourselves there.

At the end of the estate was a small paper shop, a supermarket, a wool shop, hairdressers, a chip shop and a laundrette. The laundrette was a good place to hang out. There would usually be plenty of kids

Helena Denton

in there, until an adult would chase us out so they could do their washing in peace. We didn't mind as we always had places to go. Another favourite was the chippy, where us kids would save our pennies and buy a whole load of pickled onions. We would then see who could eat the most in the shortest time. I never won this, as four would be my limit. However our Sheila was often the champion, as she hated to be beaten by anyone, and for this everyone admired her.

I couldn't help thinking this was the best estate in the whole wide world; what else could you want?

My mum was brilliant at the sewing machine and she could put her hand to anything, although my sisters and I didn't always appreciate this. She would make us clothes out of leftover material. This meant we would have to wear two-toned brightly coloured trousers and knitted jumpers.

Many times we would wear clothes she had seen in magazines and copied the designs. She told us that we looked different, not like all the other children. But we didn't want to stand out, but be normal. We just wanted to be like all the other kids and wear T-shirts and jeans. We did not have any choice in the matter; what mum said we had to obey, whether we liked it or not.

I remember I was made to wear a pair of trousers with a blue and pink section going down from the knees. They were horrid. Sue and Sheila also had

Meet Me by the Monkey Bars

to wear similar items. Some of the other children would laugh at us, but they would soon stop when Sheila threatened to beat them up. She was a year younger than me, but what a toughie! and everyone knew it.

Anyway back to those trousers, I decided there was no way I would wear them. So I spent the whole day sliding down the grass bank on my knees, trying to ruin those horrible trousers, but to my horror the material was so strong they wouldn't tear. Soon however I was having so much fun the trousers were the last thing on my mind.

On top of the bank was a group of houses, which were out of bounds; these were the "posh people". Sue and Sheila and a couple of other children decided to go over the wall of one of these houses, to have a look around their massive garden. I was on lookout duty— typical!

They seemed to be gone ages and it was becoming very boring. I decided that I was going to climb up, after all, why should I miss out on the fun? Well, climbing wasn't my strong point, and I got stuck half way. I found I couldn't go up or down, and I was getting quite tearful.

Suddenly, a man appeared from nowhere, and started to shout at me. Well that was the shock I needed, and slid down painfully down the wall. I was truly frightened and ran all the way home crying. Sue and Sheila had been at home ages and

Helena Denton

had already started their tea. They had forgotten about me. Mum looked at me and said, "Look at your trousers." My trousers had been ripped right across the knees. I was very happy until mum said, "I'll put a patch on it," and my sisters burst into fits of laughter, to my utter horror!

Chapter Two

Mum and Dad worked long hours in hotels, this meant we all had to do our jobs in the house. Sue had to make us something to eat, I had to wash the dishes, and Sheila had to sweep the floor. We were all taught to make our beds from an early age.

Mum worked in the Savoy Hotel, next to the fire station. When she heard the sirens she would always breathe a sigh of relief if it turned right, however if it went the other way she would phone us up to make sure we were okay.

If it was the weekend and we were not at school we had even more jobs to do. Sometimes when friends came to see if we were playing outside, they were amazed, as they didn't have to do anything in their own houses.

Helena Denton

One day mum was at work as usual when some friends came knocking for us to come out to play. We knew we couldn't go out unless our work was finished, so we invited them in. At first we all got stuck in, but soon it got boring and we were bit embarrassed and cheesed off, knowing that they weren't expected to do any work at home.

So we decided to have a pillow fight; Sue, Sheila Carol on one team and Margaret and I on the other team. We had our record player blasting Bay City Rollers (Sue's choice as she was the oldest). We were having the time of our lives, jumping on the beds and the feathers of the pillows were everywhere, making a real mess. I was laughing so much tears of joy were streaming down my face. I felt so free and happy, the music was blaring and we were singing at the top of our voices; it sounded like a cat's choir.

Time just flew by; suddenly mum came charging in, screaming in Portuguese. It was a good thing the others couldn't understand what she was saying, but they did know she was cross and they scampered. Sue and Sheila and I got a slipper across our bottoms.

Much to my mum's frustration, we couldn't stop laughing. It had been such a brilliant morning and no matter what, nothing was going to spoil it.

Everyone on our estate seemed to have a bike, well that is, except us. No matter how much we pleaded, mum and dad said they could not afford it. We used to watch the other children on their bikes and be green with envy.

One day there was great excitement, a boy called Maurice had been given a brand new bike. I couldn't believe it, it was the red chopper bike I had seen in a magazine — the one I wanted, it wasn't fair.

Maurice's bike was gleaming, and had silver handlebars with black rubber grips on the ends. There was a long black seat, which looked as though it was meant for a king. The rest of the bike was covered in shiny red paint and the wheels had red reflectors on them. It was so lovely I wanted it; I was so jealous. Everyday I watched Maurice polish his bike; nobody was even allowed near it.

A couple of weeks later dad told us he had a bike for us. We had a total shock — in the garage was a blue bike, well I think it was blue, it had hardly any of the paint left on it, just rust. The seat was ripped, and the front wheel was crooked. What an eyesore. Someone had thrown it away and dad had rescued it.

At first the other kids laughed, that is until Sue went on it (first always as she was the oldest). As she was going down the hill the wheel fell off. Sue had to dive off very quickly, as she could have had a serious injury. Typical dad, he had brought a bike which someone had thrown out as rubbish.

Helena Denton

Then a miracle happened. Maurice offered his brand new bike to us if he could ride ours. Suddenly we were the most popular children on the estate; everyone wanted to go on our bike. They would zoom down the hill and then jump off before the wheel came off. Sometimes they misjudged it and would be thrown off and have large bruises, but they thought it was brilliant. A queue would form to ride our bike.

I learnt to ride Maurice's bike. I loved that bike. If the world had stopped then, it wouldn't have mattered. I was the happiest kid, and nothing else would ever come close to it.

My sisters and I had the time of our lives on Maurice's bike. Everyone was having a fun time on our bike, so we were all happy.

How the kids loved our bike; I don't know who was having the most fun. It was a sad day when the bike was batterered beyond belief and when one of the mothers complained to my dad about the state of the bike and the large cut her son had received whilst riding on our bike. Dad had no choice but to throw it on the skip. I am sure I saw a tear in Maurice's eye when it was dumped. Well I thought, no more chopper rides. To Maurice's credit he still shared his bike, and we could go on it whenever we wanted to. I was forever grateful.

On his next birthday he got a new bike and gave us his old chopper bike, but not even his brand

Meet Me by the Monkey Bars

new bike could ever compete with that brilliant chopper bike. We rode on that bike until it dropped to pieces. No other bike could ever come close, it was pure magic.

Chapter Three

Every day at Troy Court was an adventure; I wouldn't know if I was going to be building a new tree-house or making a den in some secret hideaway. I don't know who told us kids to meet by the monkey bars (this was a small metal barrier, to stop the kids running straight onto the road) but everyone knew it was the meeting place; at anytime there would be somebody there.

It was so exciting, some days we would play Rounders and have the whole estate there, even the big 'cool' kids would join in the fun. Other days it would be one or two kids, just chatting.

One day it was so unusual, no one could decide what to do. Every time a suggestion was made someone would say, "We've done that." We sat

Meet Me by the Monkey Bars

around looking at each other for inspiration, everyone was thinking really hard.

Suddenly Mark snatched the cap off one of the boy who was sitting next to him. "Right, I will throw this cap and the one it lands on has got the leargey cap and has to wear it. Then we hide and if we're caught, we get the leargey." Everyone was saying their bit, talking all at once —, the game was on.

We scattered in all directions and ran from the person who wore the cap, for once it wasn't me. There were great screams of delight, big kids and little kids, all shapes and sizes, all having a whale of a time. The game went on for about an hour before I got caught and had the leargey cap.

I was never one of the best runners, and everyone seemed to be out-running me. Suddenly I spotted Amy and ran towards her, but I didn't see a large hole in the grass, and went flying. Straight away my ankle swelled up like a balloon; I was in agony.

I shouted for Amy to help, but because I still wearing the cap she thought it was a trick. She ran off, she didn't want the leargey and thought I was trying to trick her. I probably would have done the same, we were always playing tricks on each other.

There was nobody around so I hobbled home. I was crying with the pain. As I mentioned before, we lived on the top floor, every step was a nightmare.

Helena Denton

Halfway up the stairs I met two boys (the cool kids), I was so relieved to see them and thought they would help me. How wrong I was. The boys started to laugh and tease me. One of the boys, called Phil, was particularly cruel, calling me "hop-along" and blocking my path for several minutes. I was crying and managed to push past. "I will laugh my socks off when it happens to you!" I shouted at him.

Anyway, I managed to get home. Dad took me to hospital; luckily my ankle was only badly sprained, with no broken bones.

A year later there was a lot of excitement; Phil was going to be picked for the local football team. He had been in the Jersey Evening Post; a whole page was dedicated to his talent. Maybe he was to be the next Manchester United star.

If he had been one of the cool kids before, his head was now twice the size, and he thought he was even more important than any one else. How I despised him. What a show-off.

One Saturday morning whilst we were out playing I saw him. "Big head," there he was he was, running around with the ball doing his tricks. Everyone was cheering him on and he loved every minute of it. Even I had to admit he was pretty good and worth watching. Suddenly someone tackled him and he went flying. We all heard a large cracking noise. It went deadly silent— until Phil let out a piercing scream, which seemed to echo around the whole estate. It was obvious as he bit into his lip that he was trying to stop himself from crying.

Phil was rushed to the hospital. Later we heard that he had broken two bones in his leg. He wouldn't be playing football for a while. Everyone felt sorry for him, but not me, I had great delight calling him "hop-along". He looked at me and knew where I was coming from. What goes around comes around. Ha, ha. From then on Phil never teased me; so something good came out of it

Chapter Four

One Saturday afternoon there was just my friend Anna and I who seemed to have nothing in particular to do, everyone else was either making dens or busy with other games. It was obvious that they didn't want us to join in with them.

We wandered around bored, life wasn't fair. We walked along to some other children who were playing Rounders. They wouldn't let us play, saying, "Why do we want slow coaches like you?" They had a point, we were terrible runners, but I thought they were wicked. Anna and I walked off, dragging our feet.

Nobody wanted or needed two extra players. Everyone seemed to be doing something. Some were playing 2 Balla this was the name given for the two tennis balls thrown against the wall whilst singing songs, Chasey, Hopscotch, or doing handstands (well I didn't even ask to join in with that, I was never good at it).

We decided to go and feed the swans at the reservoir at the end of the estate. I couldn't believe the cheek of the swans though, even they didn't want us near them. We were "Billy-no-mates" that day.

We thought, well that's it, so we decided to go home. I was feeling very sorry for myself and looking down at my feet. Then I saw it the thing that was about to make our whole day feel different.

I started rubbing my eyes; just in case it was a trick — there lying on the ground was a buddle of £1.00 notes. There were five altogether. Anna and I thought we had found GOLD! What a stroke of luck.

Suddenly there were a few children around us. I hid the money quickly in my pocket; they weren't getting any of it. Isobel, one of the children, wanted us to play Bulldog. "No we're busy," I said. I could feel the lovely money in my pocket, and we ran off before they asked any questions.

Anna and I ran off towards the river bank; after making sure no one was about I took out the money and looked at it. I looked at it again, and then I looked at Anna. We started to jump up and down; we felt that we would explode with happiness.

Helena Denton

We started naming all the sweets we could we could buy:
Sherbet Dips
Whiz Sticks
Penny Dainties
Humbugs
Cough Candy Twists
Strawberry Shoe Laces
Cannon Balls
Juicy Lucies
Gobstoppers
Bubblegum
Bazooka Joes

The list was endless. As we named each one our eyes danced with excitement, and our mouths dribbled with the anticipation of eating whatever we wanted. We hugged each other and felt overwhelming joy.

We decided that we couldn't be seen together in the shop, in case anyone asked us why we had so much money. Anna was to go in the paper shop and I was to go in the supermarket. I had three pounds and Anna had two.

In the supermarket my mouth went dry; I had to lick my lips constantly. I carefully selected my goodies, but I don't know how I paid for my stash of goodies. I felt scared, excited, and naughty all in one go.

I carried my overflowing carrier bag to the monkey bars where I was to meet Anna. Sue and Sheila and a couple of others were there. I was terrified that I would be caught out.   Luckily they were too busy balancing upside down to notice I was there. Anna came and I gave her a secret nod and we ran off to the river bank, where we sat behind the biggest tree to hide, making sure nobody could see us.

Anna had bought two comics, *Twinkle* and *Beano*, several bars of chocolate, a large bottle of coke, two packets of Sherbet Dips, 20p of green Gobstoppers and a packet of Flying Saucers.

I had a large family size packet of cheese and onion crisps, two packets of chocolate biscuits, a quarter pound of Cough Candy Twists, Opal Fruits; two jam doughnuts and several other sticky sweets.

At first we just looked at each other, then we were ripping the wrappers off and stuffing the delicious treats into our mouths. Tears of joy ran down my face. I was in pure HEAVEN.

We were there for over an hour, reading our comics and stuffing our faces; there was no need for words it was the most delightful experience and we both knew it.

We hid the remaining sweets and crisps under the tree roots and covered them with two large stones; we knew it would be safe, as we had hidden many treasures there before.

Helena Denton

When I came home mum said she had a special treat, cream buns. I felt sick and felt as if I would burst, but to refuse meant mum would have smelt a rat. So I ate the cake, but I was so bloated every mouthful was a nightmare.

That night I went to bed feeling sick but strangely very satisfied. I dreamt I was in a world made out of chocolate, the trees were liquorice and the green grass was chewing gum. A vivid dream which was nearly as good as the real thing.

Chapter Five

Mum was one of the lucky ones who had a washing machine. Other mums would take huge bags to the laundrette. Mum said that it was her best luxury item, bought with the money she saved at the co-op weekly.

Mum would wash the clothes first by hand and give them a big wash in the washing machine. One of her proudest moments was when Sheila came home and told her that her teacher said Sheila's socks were the cleanest in the class and she was always well presented. This was like giving my mum a gold medal; it was the best compliment she could get.

Although we had a washing machine we still had to take the sheets and other large items to the laundry shed. This was a large hut with wooden air vents around the room. There were washing lines through to the end of the room. Each flat was responsible for their own laundry and would have their own pegs and baskets as well as a key to lock up, in order to keep their washing safe.

The laundry room was always filled with long lines of wet washing, which the huge fans in the ceiling would dry. The air was filled with the smell of damp clothes, a mixture of soap smells. Some of them still lingered with sweaty smells from not being washed properly; mum would always go as far away as possible from these. I would often laugh at the ladies' knickers and men's underpants on the lines. Mum would always say they should be kept private.

One washing day mum sent me to the laundry shed with two large bags of sheets, with strict instructions on how to hang the sheets properly so they wouldn't touch the floor.

As I passed the monkey bars there were two of my friends, Anna and Amy; they decided to come with me. I carefully hung the sheets with the utmost care, as I knew that mum would be most annoyed if she had to wash them again.

We decided to play 'In and out of Dusty Bluebells'. The game was to run amongst the sheets and hide while the others tried to find you.

Meet Me by the Monkey Bars

It was Anna's turn. This was a very hot game; we would run in and out of the sheets. My hair started to stick to my face with the heat; I was really red. My heart was pondering with excitement. As I could hear Anna coming nearer to me, she was singing:

"In and out of dusty bluebells,
Who will be my leader?
Pit pat on my shoulder,
Who will be my leader?
In and out of dusty bluebells."

As her voice became louder, I dodged amongst the sheets. I was very hot and sticky. The sheets began to cling to me. The more I moved, the more tangled I became. The sheets clung to my face; I felt like I couldn't breathe. I started to panic and started to scream. I felt all alone, trapped, whilst the sheets danced like white ghosts. I screamed again; then everything went black.

The next thing I knew Anna and Amy were dabbing pillowcases in my face. They looked scared as they told me that I had collapsed. I looked down at the white sheet around me. It was covered in blood — my blood. I'd had a nose bleed.

I must have fainted with the heat. We decided to get out quickly, and I went for a drink of water. I was relieved to get out of that sickly heat.

Helena Denton

After changing my T-shirt, which was covered in blood, for some reason I threw it out of the window. Later that day mum came to collect her sheets. She came back saying, "Somebody naughty has ruined a lady's washing; there was blood all over all over her washing and it had been left on the floor. If it had been mine, I would have been annoyed too." Then she handed me my T-shirt, all clean, with no blood on it!

Next day there was a sign on the laundry shed: NO CHILDREN ALLOWED WITHOUT SUPERVISION.

I was quite scared over the episode, and was glad to see the sign; this was so mum wouldn't tell me not to go in there. A couple of nights after, I had bad dreams, about ghosts trying to pull my eyes out. I would wake up terrified and go into Sheila's bed for comfort.

Even now the smell of soap powder brings back the ghosts!

Chapter Six

Each night we three girls had to be washed and in our nighties by the end of Coronation Street, and then off to bed. Sue always complained that she thought she should stay up later, but it fell on deaf ears, and we were all in bed by eight o'clock each night.

One summer was different. Sue's bed was moved into our bedroom. We were told her room was "out of bounds." This caused great excitement and curiosity. Next day a small Portuguese lady arrived with a large suitcase, and we were told not to make much noise, as she was staying with us for a while (in fact she stayed all of July and most of August).

Sue was really miffed, she didn't want some stranger staying in her room. She moaned that she didn't want to share our room, but I did notice that she moved my bed from under the window and put hers there instead. "I am the oldest," was the excuse I would often hear when she wanted her own way.

Laudvina was the lady's name. She was small and always wore black. Her hair was scraped into a tight bun. She didn't speak a word of English and was constantly clapping her hands when she thought we were making too much noise. What cheek; it was our house not hers. One good thing was that Laudvina also worked in a hotel and she would always bring eggs home. So dad would make terrific omelettes. My sisters got sick of eating eggs, but I could have eaten them until they came out of my ears, so I was happy.

My parents and Laudvina would sometimes talk very loudly while we were trying to watch TV. When we complained dad told us to play outside. We were shocked, it was past 8.30 and he hadn't noticed the time. Well, we weren't going to spoil this bit of luck so we rushed out before he realised.

It was pretty dark outside, none of our usual friends were out – probably in bed I suppose? Standing by the garages were two boys, Marc and Rui; they were surprised to see us. They started to tell us how the woods were haunted and monsters lived there.

Meet Me by the Monkey Bars

I was terrified but Sue thought it sounded great. "Show us then," she said. Wow she was really brave, I thought. I wanted to go home, I was frightened. What if the monster chased us? Or worse still ate us for supper? I didn't want to go home alone either, so I went along with them.

The woods were unrecognisable at night. I thought I knew every tree and nook and cranny of the woods, but it looked different now. The trees were odd shapes and they looked bigger, darker, and very strange.

Marc and Rui took us up to the top of the woods. It sounded different, no birds singing, very eerie, too quiet, and spooky. I stayed close to Sue. I thought my sisters were really brave.

As we walked deeper into the woods the boys told us a spooky story, about a monster with thousands of eyes, which only came out at certain times—when it was full moon. I looked at the sky, and saw the full moon; a shiver ran down my back.

The boys picked two sticks up from the ground. We were now rooted to the spot. I thought maybe they were the monsters and were going to beat our brains out. We girls were terrified.

Marc and Rui started to bang the trees with their sticks. Suddenly the woods was filled with screeching sounds. The trees were moving; they were coming towards us. I looked up and saw millions of red eyes. The creatures were swooping down over our heads. I was petrified. We started screaming and ran as fast as we could; for once my legs ran faster than my sisters'. We didn't stop until we got home.

Next day Marc and Rui were telling anyone who would listen how we thought that the bats were monsters and thought we would be eaten alive. Sue was annoyed and thought it was a right show-up.

Next night dad allowed us out late again. This time Sue had a brilliant idea. Armed with a tape recorder which we had taped noises from the TV, we hid behind the garages, and knew that Marc and Rui would be down soon for sly ciggie. We waited until they had been sitting for a while and then we turned on the spooky noise. At first they pretended they hadn't heard and tried to be cool. As the noises grew louder they panicked, and ran for their lives.

We just creased up in fits of laughter. Who says revenge isn't sweet?

Chapter Seven

One day I went to the monkey bars and Amy was there with a teenage girl. The girl had long lovely ringlets in her hair. She had a beautiful freckled face and a huge grin. She seemed like a model from the Jackie Magazine; she fascinated me. She wore tight-fitting jeans with a small cropped top, and pink high-heeled shoes. I felt quite ashamed of my home-made trousers and bright wool jumper.

Amy introduced me to Dee, her cousin, who was from Scotland. When Dee spoke I was amazed how lovely she sounded. I didn't know what she was saying, but it sounded like poetry.

Sue and Sheila joined us and Amy explained that Dee was here with her family and they were going to a wedding. I just stood there open- mouthed.

Helena Denton

When she spoke everything was, "Wee this," and "wee that." Eventually I said to her, "You can use our toilet. I know you want to go," because I had heard her say "wee" a few times. Sue hit me hard on the arm and told me not to be so silly. (Well how was I supposed to know wee meant small?!) Dee smiled and said, "Ah leave the wee bairn alone." I hadn't a clue what she meant, but I knew it was okay, because she patted me on the head.

Next day Dee was dressed in a long demin dress with a pink belt and a matching bag with a denim stripe running through it. Even her shoes matched her outfit; she looked stunning. Her hair was now really straight; I asked her if her hair was real. I couldn't believe how someone could look so different. Behind her were two little girls; well I thought they were girls, they both had tartan skirts on. I was shocked when she introduced me to her brother, "This is Craig." "But he's wearing a skirt," I said. Dee laughed and said, "It's not a skirt, it's a kilt." The other child was called Natalie. (Craig and Natalie were names I later chose for my own children, as I thought they were beautiful names.)

Dee and Amy's dads came down the stairs next and they were wearing skirts too, sorry, kilts! I was so shocked and stood there with my mouth open. Then the women came down; they all had matching blue tartan on, but they weren't a patch on the men's clothing. I couldn't decided if the men were brave or stupid.

Then I heard a loud screeching noise. I turned around and saw the old granddad also wearing a kilt, with a large sack with three pipes coming out of it. He was squeezing it under his arms and a high pitched sound was coming out of it. Sue said, "That's the bag pipes." I was amazed she knew so much. I had had never seen anything like this in my whole life.

Dee's dad shouted, "Hoy oot!" and he and all the men started to throw money into the air. There seemed to be thousands, (ok I'm exaggerating) of children running from all directions, and before I had a chance to pick any up of the coins, all the other children had collected all the money and I had none. Dee noticed and had a word with her dad. "Helena, hoy oot!" he cried, and threw a fifty pence piece in my direction, which I excitedly caught. All the other children were jealous, including my sisters, as they had only caught coppers (pennies). It was ages before I spent that money, I was so proud.

Chapter Eight

In Jersey one of the good things is the hot weather; however one of my vivid memories was when it snowed. I remember my dad telling me to get up. I looked at the clock to see it was only 7.30 a.m., what was dad playing at it? It was Saturday, no way was I getting up! I pulled the covers over my head to drown out his persistent wailing, but dad went on and on.

Dad continued until we got out of bed, me being last. I was very grumpy that I had to get out of my lovely warm bed. Dad had better have a good reason!

Had dad gone completely bonkers? Every window was wide open, and it was so cold. Then it struck me how bright everything was. It had snowed during the night and now a lovely blanket of snow covered all the grassy areas.

Well there was no stopping us now, it was a race to get dressed. Less than 10 minutes later we were out in the snow, joined by all the other children, who also wanted to be out on this wonderful morning.

That morning we made snowmen, in all shapes and sizes. We rolled down the hill; we lay in the snow, making angels. This was brilliant, we were having loads of fun.

The snowballs went in every direction. I always got hit, as I never could dodge the snowballs and became a good target. I didn't mind though as I threw as hard as the next person, and I would scream in triumph if my shot managed to hit my target, slosh straight into their face.

The river bank was so slippery, it became appealing as we grabbed a plastic bag (no one had sledges, because it didn't snow) to slide down the hill. Well that is Sue and Sheila did, they had many go's before I dared to try. When I finally went down everybody laughed as I screamed all the way down. I was terrified at the speed I was going. I have to admit I was a right scaredy cat.

After a rather shaky start, I was soon queuing up for my next turn, and having the time of my life. The laughter and screams of enjoyment ran around

Helena Denton

the whole estate. Everyone had bright rosy cheeks and a sparkle in their eyes.

We were all enjoying ourselves sliding, rolling, and mucking about. Then one by one our mothers called us in for dinner. We were having so much fun, and didn't want to leave. I think I ate my dinner in two minutes flat, much to my mum's annoyance. Then we were right back out again.

Soon we were out in the snow, with our plastic bags, going down the slope. The snow was icy now making it even faster, if I was terrified before I was even more scared than ever. With the shouts of "Chicken!" it was now my go.

I know now you should always trust your instinct. I was feeling that I really didn't want to go down. The others started to chant, "Chicken, chicken, chicken, Helena's chicken." I sat down on the plastic bag and someone gave me an almighty push. I closed my eyes and screamed and screamed as I was whizzing down the bank at a horrendous speed. Suddenly I crashed into a tree. Well at least I had stopped.

I then heard screaming all around me and looked around. What were they screaming for? The ground had a red stream running through it; what a lovely colour it looked in the white snow. Suddenly I relealised it was my blood! I had split my head open on the tree.

Meet Me by the Monkey Bars

I was taken like a wounded soldier down the slope. Then dad took me to hospital, where I had three stitches. I cried my eyes out, but soon cheered up when everyone wanted to see my wound, and I was able to recall with great exaggeration the pain of having stitches put in. For a while I felt like a hero. It lasted for two days, until Anna broke her arm and had a real injury. Trust her to steal my limelight!

Chapter Nine

I had a secret treasure box, which I hid under my bed. To anyone else it would seem like rubbish. Every time I opened my toffee box, which had a lovely picture of Corbiere Lighthouse, I felt happy. (I never got to eat the toffees though, dad had found the empty box left by one of the guests at the hotel.) I was very lucky that I had seen the box first, otherwise Sue would have claimed it for her pencils, or Sheila would have filled it with some creepy crawlies.

The first thing I always touched was a lump of silver paper, inside was bubblegum. I would place the bubble gum in my mouth; at first it was hard, but I would chew it until I counted to thirty, then it would be soft again. I had planned to keep this bubblegum forever, and enter it in 'Record

Meet Me by the Monkey Bars

Breakers'. I'm sure Roy Castle would have been well impressed.

Next I would come across a Bazooka wrapper, which had a cartoon strip, and would laugh at the funny people with their big feet. Then I would laugh at the two jokes:

Q "What goes black, white, black, white?
A A penguin rolling down the hill.

Q "What goes black, white red, red, red?
A A penguin rolling down the hill with a razorblade.

Q "What's yellow and bites?
A Shark-infested custard!

I would kill myself laughing, they never failed to amuse me! I would carefully fold the Bazooka paper whilst remembering the wonderful day Anna and I had when we found £5.00 and had our secret stash of sweets and goodies.

Next I would pick up a glass eye. This eye belonged to my beloved teddy. I would look at this bear, he was about 10 inches long and filled with sawdust; he had black ears, a stitched nose, and of course just one beady eye. I loved this bear. Even though he was badly stitched up with blue wool, to stop his stuffing falling out. I kissed my bear. "Peter, one day you will have your eye back...but not today,"

Helena Denton

I'd say to him, and then put the glass eye back in the box.

Next I picked up a cat made from a toilet roll, it was covered in green fur and filled with chickpeas. It didn't look as perfect as the one made by Blue Peter; they had black and white fur; but mum didn't have any, so green it was. It had wonky ears but looked cute, and I planned to send a photo of it to Blue Peter to get a badge.

A conker on a string caught my eye. I gave it a polish on my T-Shirt and it shone. I loved this conker; it was really shiny and in a shape of a heart. The string was tatty but I could still smell the faint smell of vinegar, which Sheila had used some months back. It was really Sheila's winning conker, but because all mine had split within seconds of playing, I claimed hers. I dreamt of being a Conker Champion. It would go back in the box.

I would then pick up notebook, which had a secret code:

*+^^^""++**_____******===+++^^
^^***********++++###***---_*

The problem was I no longer knew what it meant, as I had lost the piece of paper which could translate the code. I kept the book though, in case it came on the TV programme again: 'Why don't you switch

Meet Me by the Monkey Bars

off your television and do something less boring instead?'

Which I thought was a stupid title. If you turned your TV off you wouldn't know what they were saying.

There was a blue piece of paper, on which Sue had drawn a little family of furry creatures, wearing tartan hats. Mac Daddy, Mac Mummy, Mac, Mac Lucy and their dog Mac Fluff. Sue was very talented and would come up with these designs to keep us amused whilst mum and dad were at work.

There were numerous other stones and sticks, or anything I thought was interesting also went in this box. I would always place the items back with the utmost care.

I called this 'My Goodie Gumdrop Box'. If ever I felt bored or unhappy this box would soon cheer me up.

One day I came in and mum was going on about how messy my room was; she told me that she had spent an hour tidying it up. Good for her, I thought, one less job for me.

It wasn't until a couple of hours later I went to put a Roman coin, which probably belonged to an emperor, or someone like that, in my box. Looked under my bed and all the cupboards, still I couldn't

Helena Denton

find it. I started to panic. "Mum where's my box?!" I shouted.

I couldn't believe it; she had thrown it out. My treasures had gone! I would no longer be on the Record Breaker with my long-lasting Bubblegum, or get a Blue Peter badge for my cat. As for my teddy bear, he still sits on my bed today, looking at me with his one beady eye. I changed his name to 'One Eye Jack', it seemed more suitable.

Chapter Ten

When we weren't playing outside we would be playing indoors, either drawing or watching TV. Dad and mum didn't believe that children should have many toys, they thought children should be able to entertain themselves. So the toys we did have we appreciated, and took great care of them.

I remember having a game called Jack Straws; it was a load of instruments and work tools made out of yellow plastic; they came in a small box. The point of the game was to throw the straws (silly name as there weren't any straws in it!) and then you had to pick them up with a long needle, without moving the others. I spent many good hours entertaining myself with this game. It especially came in useful when Sue and Sheila had fallen out with me.

Helena Denton

I always thought Sheila was very lucky as she always had a partner— either Sue or myself, and on good days both, so she always had someone to play with.

The three of us loved books, which we would borrow from the library, and we would read them from start to finish in a couple of days. Sue would read any classics that came to her hand, such as 'Jane Eyre.' Sheila would always have a story containing some kind of animal. I would read Enid Blyton stories, which I loved, and imagine I was that character, my favourite being The Naughtiest Girl in School, because she was so wicked. The books we were reading would become useful when mum wanted us to do some extra housework, we would claim that we needed to finish them because they were part of our homework. As she was a great believer in good schooling, she would leave us be.

Like any other children we would love to sit in front of the TV. It was great when mum and dad were out we could watch TV in peace. However if mum was around, if we were watching 'Tarzan', as soon as the crocodiles or snakes came on mum would turn over to the other channel, screaming she couldn't watch it because it frightened her. So by the time we had turned back to the film we had missed the best bit or had lost the plot of the story. Or when it came to 'Angels'— about a hospital drama, as soon as an operation started, or somebody came in covered with blood, mum would get squeamish and tell us to turn over, so we rarely got to see the complete programme.

One day dad caused great excitement; he was taking the whole family to the cinema. This was a rare treat. The only problem was the film was 'Carry On Girls.' Dad laughed out really loud every time vast amounts of boobs were displayed. Dad laughed even louder when Barbara Windsor appeared and her ample bosom was shown. Every time Kenneth Williams came on dad would boo as loud as he could; for some reason dad hated the way he spoke. We cringed at how loud dad was being. Just as well none of our friends would know, as they were never allowed to see a film like this.

So we girls would be cringing in our seats; as dad's voice got louder his voice seemed to echo around the room, how embarrassing. Mum just sat there stone-faced. When the film finally finished mum gave dad a right dressing down, "Fancy taking us to see women parading in their underwear!" She gave dad the silent treatment for the rest of the day. However dad didn't notice, much to mum's annoyance; he was too busy doing impressions of Sid James – with a Portuguese accent, somehow he sounded nothing like him!

One night Sue noticed there was a Frankenstein film late on TV. She really wanted to see it. Sue thought up a plan. Near bedtime we started to talk constantly while mum and dad were trying to watch one of their mundane programmes. Dad

Helena Denton

said, "Bedtime." Sue replied, "Good, I couldn't stay up even if I wanted to," and she gave an exaggerated yawn. Dad caught the bait. "Right you can stay up all night and watch the scary programmes, but no moaning." Sue rushed to the kitchen, grabbing a whole load of goodies, and then made herself very comfortable in the best seat in the living room.

When 'Frankenstein' came on mum went to bed. I sat with a cushion over my face, I was terrified and jumped at the slightest noise. My sisters were having a whale of time, really engrossed in the film, and weren't frightened in the least.

However dad kept saying, "You can go to bed anytime you want," but my sisters insisted they watch it from start to finish. When it had finished dad told us, "Don't come running to my bed when you have nightmares." I was so tired I didn't have time for nightmares and my sisters each slept like a log.

However mum had great delight in telling us that dad had had nightmares. He was being attacked by monsters, which turned out to be giant rats.

His dream was linked to when he was younger, about fourteen. He had been working in restaurant which had a field nearby; this is where he fed the rats. One day he was outside but had no food. A large rat jumped onto his leg and bit him; its jaws locked onto my dad's knee. The restaurant owner heard my dad's screams, he grabbed a large

Meet Me by the Monkey Bars

plank of wood and started to hit the rat. The rat refused to budge, and dad was screaming in pain. After several painful minutes the rat finally let go. Dad had to be rushed to hospital and given a rabies needle in his bottom (which he said hurt like hell!).

As a result we were never allowed to stay up and watch horror films again until we were old enough to sit by ourselves.

Other times to entertain us dad would put on the records he had been given by guests from the hotel, who did not want to carry them back home. There were several Elvis, Cliff Richard, and Tony Christie. We would all sing along, but it would always end up with some Portuguese folk singer. This was our cue to go to bed, as they all seemed to be screeching; when you heard one you heard the lot.

Sometimes Sue would put her Bay City Rollers on, although I liked them I pretended that I didn't, so I could have the Osmonds on with Marie and Donny singing 'Paper Roses'. As it was Sue's record player she always won and we three would go to bed singing, "Shang Lang Shang Lang."

Chapter Eleven

Mum was always cooking. There would be large pans of stew with rice and peas, or dried salty cod, which had been stored on a large hook in the cupboard. Or she would have a pan filled with lots of vegetables chopped up and boiled into a thick broth.

There was always a pan on the stove ready to be heated up; as mum and dad worked different shifts this meant they could eat anytime they came back from work.

Mum was very understanding, knowing that I wouldn't eat rice, stew, vegetables or even her home-made soup. I lived on eggs, chips or hotdogs. Mum would always cut potatoes into chips and did what she called "English food". She didn't mind as

Meet Me by the Monkey Bars

long as I was eating. The table would always have fresh bread, which she brought from the market.

One day I had finished school and dad was there making dinner that night. He had a large pot with boiled rice, green beans and red peppers and another pan with courgettes. I reminded him that he had to cook something else for me. "One of your lovely omelettes," I told him. Usually this would have been no problem as he would agree, but dad took no notice this time, and I realised he was in one of his grumpy moods.

He served the rice and the courgettes leaving my plate empty. I wasn't worried, as I knew he could make an omelette as quick as a flash.

Dad then placed the rice and two large courgettes on to my plate. I sweetly reminded him about my omelette. Dad started to rant and rave saying that we were Portuguese and I should eat what I was given. I was never one to keep my mouth shout and told him that he should never have come here to Jersey if he couldn't accept change. Also that I was not Portuguese as I had been born in Jersey so I should eat what I liked.

Dad started to shout that I must eat everything on my plate, and I knew I was in for a bad time. He told me I was not to leave the table until I had eaten all my dinner. Sue and Sheila ate their dinner in silence. They knew what dad was like; he would never back down when he was in this type of mood.

Dad was very stone-faced as he ate his dinner. I sat there and looked at the rice and courgettes— it reminded me of maggots in green snots. There was no way on earth I would eat this. Dad finished his dinner. My sisters gave me a sympathetic look. After they had finished they left me, knowing they couldn't help as there was nothing they could do.

The more dad got annoyed the more I stood my ground; I was not going to eat it. The rice was now stone cold and stuck to the plate; it had been half an hour since my dad had put my dinner down and I was even more determined, but so was my dad.

Dad was getting angrier by the minute, I am sure he would have force-fed me if the telephone hadn't rung at that moment. He warned me not to throw away the food, as he would check the bin. I sat there with tears running down my cheeks.

Then Sue and Sheila came in with two plastic bags and scraped the rice and courgettes into the bags, then stuffed the bags up their jumpers and went out of the kitchen without a word. To me my sisters were angels, but if dad had caught them they would have been severely punished. They had risked this to save me; I would be eternally grateful.

Dad finished his telephone call, then seeing my plate empty he checked the bin. He seemed very

Meet Me by the Monkey Bars

pleased, he thought he had won. He patted me on the head and smiled. I couldn't bear to look at him.

An hour later mum returned from work and she asked dad if we had eaten. He told her that we all ate rice and courgettes. Mum asked what I had eaten. Dad proudly told him that I had eaten the same. Mum called me in and asked me what I had eaten. I started to cry and said I had hidden the rice and there was no way I would eat it. "I hate rice, I will never eat it as long as I live!!" I shouted, and ran out of the room.

Dad then came into my bedroom with a cup of tea— his way of saying sorry. Mum followed with an extra large fried egg sandwich, good old mum.

To this day I can't stand rice, and sometimes if I go to my parents' house for dinner my dad will say with a twinkle in his eye, "Fancy some rice Helena?" "Don't you dare!" I always reply.

Chapter Twelve

At Troy Court no pets were allowed in the flats, much to Sheila's disappointment as she loved animals. Her half of the bedroom was always covered in posters: snakes, spiders, ferrets and other animals that were not the cuddly variety. After we played outside and came in mum would ask Sheila to empty her pockets, because one time mum had found five match boxes each containing little creepy crawlies. I thought she would be the next Gerald Durrell— a naturalist who saved endangered animals and created the wonderful Jersey Zoo.

If I saw a spider in the flat I would scream the place down. Then Sheila would come and rescue the spider and carefully place it outside.

Meet Me by the Monkey Bars

At one time Sheila had an animal called Molly, which she fed and talked to all the time; this was really a piece of brown fur which she kept in a brown box with holes in the lid. In the end she was so convincing that I would ask her how Molly was doing and listen with great interest about her day.

One day Dad came home with a cardboard box. We were not really interested because he always brought home what we considered as rubbish: other people's unwanted belongings from the hotel. Dad kept asking us to look in the box; he went on and on. Sheila opened the box and all she could say was "Wow!" This got our attention.

Sheila was now holding a tiny black and white kitten with huge green eyes. The kitten looked frightened, then it snuggled into Sheila's furry jumper and purred.

Dad said the cat's name was Cookinious, a Portuguese name. Sheila decided it was too long and called him Whiskers instead because of his lovely whiskers, which tickled you when it was stroked.

Susan, who was always the sensible one, mentioned the rule about no pets. Dad said no one would know because it would be a house cat.

The kitten was very funny. Whiskers kept us entertained. Even my mum (who said she didn't like animals) allowed Whiskers to pull at her tights

Helena Denton

at the toes and would laugh when the tights were stretched and pinged back, causing Whiskers to dance about excitedly. Whiskers would repeat this game until mum's tights were in tatters.

We all loved Whiskers and enjoyed playing games with him, but he was Sheila's baby and would run to her as soon as she came into sight.

Sheila boasted to anyone who would listen that we had a pet. One of the boys asked her to bring the kitten outside. Sue warned Sheila it was a silly idea, and if he didn't believe us, well tough. Sheila wasn't going to allow anyone to call her a liar. So the next day she brought down the cat in a box to show off to everyone.

Everyone wanted to hold Whiskers and he was getting very noisy. Whiskers was getting very frightened. Suddenly he jumped out of the box and ran towards a drain; he was so small he fell down between the bars. We all screamed; we thought the kitten would be killed.

Sheila tried to reach the kitten but she could only see his green eyes in the pitch black. In fact we all tried to rescue the kitten. We were all getting very upset. The boys tried to get the grate off but it was too heavy. Sheila started to cry when she heard Whiskers' distressed miaow.

It was time to go home as it was getting late, we could hear mum calling for us in the distance. We didn't want to go. Maurice, Marc, and Phil promised they would stay and get the cat out.

At home we couldn't eat our tea, we were so upset. Dad asked us where Cookinious (he still called him by the Portuguese name) was. Sue told him that the cat was hiding somewhere. Luckily he believed us.

We were not allowed out after our dinner though as dad said it was too dark. We fretted all night and there was no consoling Sheila; she was too upset.

Next morning we got up at eight o'clock (luckily it was Saturday). We ran down to the drain; we couldn't hear anything; we shone a torch down, but nothing. We had lost Whiskers forever. Sheila was in a terrible state, as she blamed herself.

Suddenly Marc, Maurice, Phil and Jack (Phil's older brother) came. Jack explained that they had managed to get the grate off after a big struggle and he now had Whiskers safely at his house.

He gave us a lecture on how we needed to treat animals with more respect. We shamefully just nodded, we had learnt our lesson. We thanked the boys and took Whiskers home. We bathed the kitten; he shook for ages; he had been through a great ordeal.

Next day dad came home with a man we hadn't seen before. He started to shout "Cookinious!"

Helena Denton

To our amazement Whiskers ran straight to him purring very loudly. Dad explained that it was his cat and we were just looking after it while he was on holiday. Sheila was furious, "You mean it wasn't our cat?!" she cried. Dad thought it was very funny. The man took Whiskers away and we girls cried for ages. We didn't speak to dad for ages. Although we did have the last laugh. Whiskers left dad a present. Dad found a lump of poo behind the TV, which he had to clean up. Serves him right.

Chapter Thirteen

One Saturday morning I was sent to the shops to buy some groceries; mum told me to take Sheila along to help carry the shopping. Sheila always claimed that the bags were too heavy though and I always ended carrying the shopping myself. So she was no help whatsoever; however I did enjoy her company as she could talk for England.

The supermarket was situated at the end of the estate. It was a mixture of corner shop and supermarket, as Jersey was getting more food from the mainland. Outside the shop were several large baskets, filled with flour, sugar, fresh fruit and vegetables, so shoppers could serve themselves.

On this day I was about to go in the shop when I noticed a small dog sniffing the brown sugar. To my horror the dog lifted his leg and peed straight into the sugar. I was amazed it hadn't changed colour. I went straight into the shop and told Mrs. C. (her name was too long to remember although I never called her this to her face). I was expecting her to be pleased, but she grabbed my arm very roughly and said, "Shut up, your mum doesn't buy it anyway."

I was very annoyed, if it was up to me I wouldn't shop there ever again, but I was more scared of what my mum would say if I came home with no shopping. First on my list was a tin of peas. There was a promotion: *PEAS HALF PRICE TODAY*. There was a huge display of tins of peas nearly reaching the ceiling, it looked amazing. I took a tin gently from the pile. As I walked away there was a huge rumble. What on earth is that? I thought. Crash!!

Every tin of peas fell down. I rushed to stop them but it was as if in slow motion. I couldn't stop it. Everyone ran around screaming. People are so dramatic, I thought. Suddenly it went deadly quiet. I looked at all the tins rolling on the shop floor.

"Look what you have done. Oh my God! Oh my God!" Mrs C. shouted. She grabbed my arm (second time that day) and shoved me out of the shop. "Wait, I haven't done mum's shopping," I said, but she just glared at me. If looks could kill... I thought.

Meet Me by the Monkey Bars

Sheila and I sat on the wall next to the shop, knowing mum would be annoyed that I hadn't done her shopping.

We started to play a game called 'Who's who'. Anyone who passed by we had to make up a name for, and make up a little story about them. The first person was a large lady wearing a blue coat; we called her Mrs. Jones and imagined that she works in a bakery and has five dogs and no kids.

Several people passed by; we were enjoying this game, describing them, but we had to whisper. I didn't want anyone to hear us and get into more trouble.

A man passed us wearing a big checked hat, a long overcoat, and dark sunglasses. We called him Mr Shifty. I said he was a spy and he was going to murder someone — yes, Mrs C. and her smelly sugar.

Mr Shifty went into the supermarket. Several minutes later he ran out with the shop's takings. He drove off in a red car. Mrs C. shouted, "We've been robbed!" as she ran after him. I just stood there amazed, my mouth wide open. This doesn't happen here... it was like in the films.

Mrs C. was now frantic; she was screaming over and over again. Sheila calmly went up to her gave her a full description of Mr Shifty and even told

Helena Denton

her the registration of the red car. How did she get that? I just stood there gob smacked.

The police were called and were very impressed with Sheila's description. Mrs C. said, "At least someone was paying attention," and looked straight at me. Sarcastic cow! Then I blushed, it was as if she read my mind, she tutted and shook her head.

Mrs. C rewarded Sheila with a £5.00 voucher to spend in her shop, this pleased mum and dad. From then on Mrs .C welcomed Sheila with open arms, but totally blanked me.

Several weeks later Mrs C. Shop had a mystery visit, then her shop was closed down, due to the fact her stock wasn't up to standard. Nobody knows who made that phone call.

The shop was later taken over by a nice family, who everybody likes, and nobody ever complained, as their shop was spotless.

Chapter Fourteen

On the second Thursday in August Jersey goes crazy. This is because of *The Battle of Flowers* - the highlight of Jersey's summer season. This always caused great excitement, not only for the visitors but also for all the locals, who had spent all their time designing and decorating wonderful floats. There would always be a big celebrity there, such as Hughie Green or Engelbert Humperdink.

No matter how much we begged, dad would not take us, because of the entry fee. He would say we could see it from a distance, but it was not the same! At the end of the procession the gates would open and everyone could see the floats. This is when we went, but the excitement had gone, so had the famous stars, and all the people dressed up

Helena Denton

were no longer there. We always felt as if we had been cheated out of a big occasion.

One August was different, we actually got in to see the parade. It was fabulous and worth the wait. The flowers and all the colours were out of this world; it was very exciting. However my dad moaned all the time, not because of the entry fee, but because a rather large lady sat in front of him with a huge white hat. Dad couldn't see a thing. He politely asked the lady to remove her hat, to which her reply was, "Certainly not, I don't want to get sunstroke." Dad swore in Portuguese and called her a fat cow, much to the amusement of the other Portuguese people in the crowd.

As usual dad had his camera with him, however when the film was developed it caused great laughter to us girls, all you could see was a large white hat obstructing the view of the floats. Dad's language was choice!

Another time we were out on our travels to see Princess Anne. She had come to unveil a plaque in Howard Davis Park. This park was a favourite with our family as we often went here when mum finished work. We would sit in this lovely park and be entertained by the live bands, ranging from jazz to military bands, all very exciting.

On this day everyone was excited, especially my mum, who was a great royal fan. We all had our Sunday best clothes on and waved union jacks.

Meet Me by the Monkey Bars

However Princess Anne had been delayed from a previous engagement and we seemed to waiting forever. It was very hot and the crowds of people were getting all hot and bothered.

I sat on the ground as I was very tired. Suddenly a roar came from the crowd and everyone pushed forward. Sue managed to pull me up just before I was trampled. Everyone was singing and cheering and waving their flags. All I could see was a lady in a navy blue suit and a cream and blue hat. When Sue told me that lady was the Princess I was really disappointed – I mean she was not wearing a crown or a ball gown, how disappointing. I felt I had been cheated.

On other days if we weren't at the park you would find our family at the beach. Mum would pack a hamper filled with chicken sandwiches in long baguettes, fresh fruit, corn on the cob, cold hot dogs and a flask of hot soup. Mum would have a huge blanket for us to sit on. Dad would have his camera again! We would have photos taken before we got to the beach and then plenty during the day (our photo albums are filled with many grumpy faces as we hated having our photos taken).

Jersey was well known for its lovely beaches; my favourite was St Brelade's Bay. The glorious sandy beach always made me feel very happy. I loved to feel the hot sand between my toes and watch the waves crash over the rocks.

Helena Denton

I had a lovely new terry towel swimsuit in bright orange. It was an all-in-one suit with a zip going down the middle, and a thin black belt across the waist.

Sue and Sheila started to make a sandcastle, but they didn't want me to help as they said I was a "snitch". Earlier that day I had reminded mum it was Sue's turn to do the dishes. Well it was either her or me, so what's a girl to do?

Playing alone I decided to go in the sea. The sea was lovely and I sat in the shallow water letting the waves lap my toes. After 10 minutes I went for a really nice swim. As I swam I felt tired and I tried to swim back to the shore, but I felt very heavy, a weird feeling; I seemed to be held back. I kept trying to come to shore but I was getting pulled back.

I started to wave to mum but she just waved back. It took a while but eventually I managed to come back safely to shallow water. I was now only knee deep but I was still struggling to get out. Then to my horror I looked down at my swimsuit, it had stretched and was now down at my toes. The swimsuit had absorbed the water like a towel and expanded.

Everybody was laughing as I tried to walk from the water's edge to where my family was sitting. Every step was a nightmare. The swimsuit was now like a long dress. For once luck was on my side, dad had run out of film, so fortunately no photos could be taken of my shame.

Sue and Sheila thought I looked very funny and couldn't stop laughing. I sat in this swimsuit with a towel around me for the rest of the day, as the swimsuit didn't regain its shape.

Mum said, "It could only happen to Helena!" Too true!!

Chapter Fifteen

Every Sunday we were dressed in our what mum called our best clothes. One Sunday I wore a red checked dress with a blue cape with bright orange lining and huge gold buttons. Sue and Sheila wore similar items. This had to be the worst day of the week, as we never felt "normal".

We walked down the stairs to the car where there would be a few of the boys standing around. One clown would always make comments like "Don't you like nice." Mum would smile and be very pleased. I couldn't believe that she couldn't hear the sarcasm in their voice. Also she never saw the way those boys held their clothes and mimicked us over our clothes, laughing at us. This always annoyed me. What a long day this was going to be. We were on the way to church.

Meet Me by the Monkey Bars

It was St Mary and Peter's Church, a large Catholic Church. Inside I would sit and stare at the beautiful glass stained windows, these were my Godsend (ha ha, a joke). I would count the different coloured glass panels to stop me falling asleep whilst Father (isn't it terrible? I can't remember his name; well just shows how interested I was in his service) delivered his sermon.

Mum would always nudge me when it was time to take the 'Body of Christ'. This always worried me because I didn't want to think about what part of his body I was eating. I was always worried it would be his bottom, and I would blush terribly when the priest came to give me the Bread of Life. As I worried about this, the priest could obviously read my mind, as he always gave me a beady eye. Whilst thinking these thoughts the priest placed the Body of Christ on my tongue. Because I wasn't quite ready I accidentally bit the priest's finger. He leaned very close and said, "Stupid little girl!" I was so shocked; he was supposed to be holier than holy.

All through the service I just sat staring at him, I couldn't believe how he could call me stupid; after all he was always preaching about being good.

At the end of the service we all lined up to shake his hand. The priest said to me, "I noticed that you were interested in my sermon today (if only he knew...) would you like to do a reading next week?" "No thank you," I replied. The priest looked like he

Helena Denton

had swallowed a wasp, he turned red and bloated, and squeezed my arm roughly. Dad stepped in and shook the priest's hand and said, "Helena would be honoured to do it."

On the way home I moaned that I wasn't going to do it. Not if I could help it, I thought. Dad told me that I had no choice in the matter. I was furious. Why didn't adults listen?!

Next Sunday came sooner than I wished. The priest handed me a long reading to look at. I didn't say a thing, I just sat there stone-faced.

The priest nodded to me, this was my sign to come to the pulpit. It went really quiet. As I started to read I pretended that I had a sore throat, and read as croakily as I could, coughing throughout. The priest was giving me daggers, half way through he asked me to stop, and got somebody else to finish the reading. I gave a smile of triumph.

At the end of the sermon everyone was coming up to me saying how brave I was reading whilst being unwell. I gave them all a cute brown-eyed look and said, "I tried, for the good of the Church."

The priest was furious. He knew I had been pretending. But before he could say anything I told him that would be the last time he ever called me stupid. He looked even angrier, but before he could say anything, I cheekily said, "Father you don't want to answer, just think how many Hail Mary's you will have to say, and you don't want that do you?"

The priest's face suddenly changed and he laughed out loud. He shook my hand warmly. Going to church didn't seem too bad after that.

However as Catholics we had to have our First Holy Communion. This was a very important day of our lives, so we kept being told! We would all be dressed in beautiful white dresses, and have a wonderful day. I had seen a wonderful white lacy dress, like a miniature wedding dress, complete with veil. Mum said she already had a dress in mind. Two weeks before our "special day" mum arrived with heavy thick cream material, which was extremely itchy. I was disappointed; this wasn't going to be the wonderful lacy, flowing dress that I had dreamed of.

Mum made three dresses, long right down to the ground, and then we had a long heavy veil; it was horrible. Sue said, "We look like nuns." Mum was pleased and said that she had asked the nuns for the pattern. We cried, we threw tantrums, but we still had to wear them. When we arrived at the church all the other girls were dressed in the miniature wedding lacy dresses that I had wanted. We looked out of place and everyone laughed at us. It was going to be another long day. Next day we were in the church newsletter. It said: *Little Costa Sisters looked heavenly in their nun outfits.* Another embarrassment in our lives. However

Helena Denton

mum and dad thought this was a great compliment, and showed the newsletter to everyone.

Sunday afternoons were just as exciting (I'm being very sarcastic, in case you haven't noticed). Dad would take us for long rides in the car, but instead of visiting all the lovely places Jersey had to offer we only had small glances of them. Dad would take us to one of the beaches and tell us to get out of the car; he would take some photos of the beautiful scenery and we would be in the photos. Before we could look around we would be piled back into the car and on to the next beauty spot.

We never really saw much of Jersey. However our photograph album showed many beautiful sights and everyone said how lucky we were to have visited these places. How could they not tell? We hated posing what seemed a hundred times; we were fed up with smiling and this showed in the tearful faces and grumpy frowns. Dad didn't care, as long as he had his photographs he was happy.

Mum always told dad at the end of each trip that we needed a treat. This would be a large ice cream. My choice was a double cone with lovely green mint ice cream with chocolate chips. Well I thought I had deserved it after all the posing we had done. It was purely delicious.

After eating our ice creams we piled back into the car. I have never been a good traveller and I always had the window opened when travelling in the car.

Meet Me by the Monkey Bars

Many times in the past I had Dad stop for me to be sick.

We had been driving a short distance. "Stop! I'm going to be sick." I shouted. Dad wasn't able to stop straight away so mum shoved a newspaper on my knee, where to my sister's disgust, I was sick.

My mum looked really worried and I was touched by her concern, but as usual I was put right. "It's not that you have been sick. Look, it's all over the Queen's face." Mum was horrified.

There had been a special pullout on the Queen, and my mum, being a true royal fan, was most upset. Dad tried to get that newspaper again but every shop had sold out because of this special feature. I still feel guilty to this day. When I see mum watching the Queen on television she always gives me a strange look, and I know she is remembering when I was sick on the Queen…I hope the Queen never finds out or it will be off with my head!

Chapter Sixteen

Christmas and birthdays were always celebrated by having practical presents such as clothes or school equipment, never exciting toys, like the rest of the children on our estate had.

One birthday before I was due to go to Secondary school there was huge present for me. It was wrapped in red shiny paper. Just as I was about to open it mum told me not to tear the paper as she wanted to keep the paper for another occasion. Although I was dying to rip it open, I carefully unpeeled the cellotape. It seemed to take ages. When I finally opened it I was truly and utterly disappointed; inside was a hockey stick and the new school uniform. Mum was very pleased and said it was a bargain by getting it so early. How was I going to tell my friends what I had been given

Meet Me by the Monkey Bars

for my birthday? They already thought we were weird.

I always thought the next birthday or Christmas would bring the new Tiny Tears doll, but it never came. Another thing that would make me mad, my dad would always say, "I don't give presents but I'll give you my blessing." I had enough blessings to last a lifetime. I wanted presents.

One January just after Sue's 12th birthday dad came home with a large carrier bag. We were quite surprised and excited, as it was from a well-known toyshop. Maybe dad had bought Sue a present.

Inside the bag was a large box 'Robbie the Robot' it said, in huge blue letters. Sue opened the box, and there was a large silver robot. The robot had a square head with flashing eyes, a big oblong body with lots of interesting buttons on it and arms with claws. It looked as if dad had spent quite a bit of money, it was really impressive.

Sue said, "Nice toy, but isn't really for a boy?" Dad told her it wasn't a present for her, but for his friend's son whose birthday it was the following week.

Sue went wild, saying that he never brought us any toys but had just brought a toy for someone he hardly knew, and it was typical of him to be showing off. She then went on to tell him that she was sick of getting his blessings and never any toys.

Helena Denton

Sheila and I just stood there with our mouths open; we would never dream of telling dad this although we wanted to many times. We waited. Sue was in big trouble now.

Dad told us to get in the car. Sue sat in a sulk and Sheila and I didn't say a word. Dad drove not saying a word, this was creepy, we didn't know what was going to happen next. I didn't have a clue what dad would do next, and more to the point where was he taking us.

After 10 minutes dad stopped the car outside the toyshop. He told us that we could have a present each. The shop was wonderful, filled with all the dolls, teddies, cars, stuffed animals and every toy a child could ever dream of.

I stared for ages, just looking around, as if it had been my first time in this shop. I was in a trance but brought quickly to my senses with a nudge in the ribs from Sue. "Quick before dad changes his mind. Grab something you idiot."

Sue got a pair of roller skates. Sheila got a large bag of zoo animals and a Snakes and Ladders game. I didn't know what to get. "Five minutes to closing," the announcement was heard throughout the shop. Sue grabbed my hand, "Quick!" I picked a Fuzzy Felt Hospital Set and an Enid Blyton book. Sheila and I pushed our luck by getting two presents because we knew Dad wouldn't challenge it.

Meet Me by the Monkey Bars

At the counter the lady said to dad, "Oh what a nice man you are, buying presents for your children." Dad replied, "Yes I like to spoil them, my lovely daughters." Usually we girls would have cringed at this type of remark, but right then we were like the cat that got the cream and we smiled at her as sweetly as we could.

Sue was very proud of her new skates. If someone had offered her a diamond necklace instead of her brand spanking new roller skates I bet she would have turned him or her down; she loved those skates.

Everyday she went on the skates; they became like her second feet. Mum would often tell her off for wearing them inside. One day she was kind enough to let me have a go. "Go on, it's easy peasy, even you can do it," Sue said.

At first I fell a few times and my balance was very shaky. Then I started to relax and it wasn't too bad. That is until I was on a small slope. Suddenly I couldn't stop, my skates were going faster and gaining speed. I had no control. I started to panic and scream; my sisters were trying their best to stop me. Suddenly I hit a curb and went flying, banging my head straight on Amy's bedroom window (ground floor).

My head hurt and I felt as if a hundred feet were trampling on my head. My sisters took me home.

Helena Denton

Mum had to fill me in on what happened during the next few hours. She told me I had fainted and dad rushed me to the hospital. I had mild concussion and had to stay overnight to be kept an eye on.

Meanwhile Amy's angry mum had come knocking at our door demanding that my mum should pay for the broken window, which I had cracked with the force of my head (although I don't remember this happening).

I slept for a whole 12 hours and then woke up and asked for a fried egg sandwich and a bar of chocolate, which I was given by the nurse, and then sent home.

When I came home I had an angry dad to face. He was not happy about having to pay Amy's mum. However it got worse. Sue came charging up to me saying she would never speak to me again as I had buckled her beloved skates. I was really upset that I had spoilt her most prized procession.

However the following week Isobel left her skates outside her front door. Sue exchanged the buckled skate for her good one. Luckily Isobel was never the wiser, although she did wonder why she seemed to drift off to the right all the time.

Isobel scored too in the end as her mum brought her top-of-the-line new roller blades. She even passed her old skates to Sheila. Everybody would laugh to see Sheila's legs go in different directions, until dad banged the skate with a hammer, then it was as good as new.

As for me, that was the first and last time ever on roller skates!

Chapter Seventeen

As I mentioned before mum and dad worked in hotels. Mum worked in the Savoy and had stayed with the same hotel for years and years. Unlike dad, who worked in many different hotels; he didn't stay more than a couple of years in the same place. He wanted to see new people and work in different areas; he had itchy feet and always wanted to go somewhere else. This was a bonus to us in the summer holidays because once week dad would take us to the new hotel where he worked; we would go through the side gate and mingle with the guests. We would use the swimming pool and eat from the buffet-style lunches.

No one ever questioned us, as everyone assumed we were some guest's children and we were free to do what we wanted. Early in the mornings

Meet Me by the Monkey Bars

we would explore the hotel and get into mischief. Our favourite pastime was to change the guests' shoes around. The guests placed their shoes in the corridors so they could be polished. We would change the shoes around making odd pairs. When the chambermaids came they had to go around and match up the shoes. We were never caught although we did come close. The housekeeper found us and asked our room number and us who our parents were. Sue pretended that we couldn't speak English and she rambled on in what seemed to be another language. The housekeeper walked away shaking her head; my that was close.

We would spend hours in the Library. This was a room in the hotel full of books which guests had read and left for other guests to read, over the years a good assortment of books had been collected.

One day whilst fully engrossed in 'Charlie and the Chocolate Factory' which had me imagining that I was eating all those wonderful sweets, and I was Charlie in that wonderful place. Sue and Sheila were also quietly reading when a man came in to the room. He looked at us and walked out. Several minutes later he returned, followed by a chambermaid, carrying a large jug of orange juice and a tray of sandwiches. He instructed her to put the tray on the table. "So you're not disturbed Miss Costas." I looked at him gob smacked; he knew who we were. "How?" I asked him. "It's my job to know everything. I am the manager!"

Helena Denton

I always thought the hotel was a very exciting place. There were always a lot of interesting people. Little old ladies with blue rinses in their hair were talking very loudly, ordering their cups of tea and sitting next to the large windows whilst playing their game of cards.

In nearby seats would be a young couple, obviously just married, by the way they could not keep their hands off each other. The young man would whisper something into the lady's ear and she would give a loud giggle and then kiss him. This would go on for several minutes until they decided to go for a walk, still hanging onto each other as they walked out of the foyer.

There were men in their business suits arranging their next meetings, ladies who love to shop, and families arguing over where to visit next. They were all fascinating. I wanted to listen to all their conversations. I would eavesdrop on the chambermaids too, who often were gossiping about somebody. It made it even more interesting when I knew who they were talking about. Sometimes they caught me listening and changed to speaking in Portuguese, but hey that was good too, as I could still understand what they were saying.

I would sit for hours in a large chair and listen to people's conversation. Everyone seemed to have an exciting life, and for a while I was in his or her lives too.

Meet Me by the Monkey Bars

At the end of the day, at about eight o'clock, dad would take us home in his car. But one day we couldn't see dad's old Vauxhall. Dad came out of the hotel and said, "I am going to pinch a car." He tried several doors of the cars in the hotel car park. Then he came to a blue Citroen and tried the door, it opened. He told us to get in the car very quickly; now saying that it was the car he always wanted.

We were terrified. Dad looked in the glove box and found some keys. He started the car and drove out of the car park. He told us if we saw a police car we had to hide in the back seat. We lay down every time a police car passed by. Sue pleaded with dad to return the car before we were taken to prison. I was now crying, I didn't want to go to prison and eat porridge. I hated porridge.

Dad then took the road to pick mum up from work. When we were at the Savoy Hotel mum opened the door of the car and looked at us three girls sitting crying hysterically. Mum demanded an explanation. "Dad stole the car and now we're going to prison." Mum looked at dad and shook her head. She went to the glove box and showed us some car papers with dad's name on it. "It's his car, he bought it today." Dad started to laugh and laugh. I think I came to the conclusion that my dad was mad!!

None of us would speak to dad, and all he kept saying was, "A joke, a joke." Yeah, but nobody was laughing.

Helena Denton

We always ended up in George's Café. This was a small café run by George and his wife Claudia, who were Portuguese like my parents.

The café had Portuguese flags around the room and red plastic tablecloths on each table. The café was a meeting place for all the Portuguese and their families. The people in there always talked loudly whilst waving their arms. My sisters and I would sit at a table away from the adults drinking our bottles of Fanta.

The café had Portuguese folk music, which we had heard a thousand times before. One day I was quite shocked; mum came downstairs wearing the traditional folk costume from Madeira. She wore a white blouse with large red multi-coloured skirt with a red waistcoat, and a small skull cap on her head.

The music was turned up loudly and all the tables were moved to the corner of the room. Everybody formed a large circle with mum in the middle. Mum started to click her fingers and stomp her feet as she danced to 'Ballerina De Madeira'. Usually mum was very reserved and would hate this attention, but here she was swinging her skirt and having a whale of time. I was quite embarrassed.

Every now and again mum was handed a glass of Madeira wine which she drank. Mum got louder and louder, everyone cheered and encouraged her. An English couple opened the café door but quickly closed it again and left; not surprising, they must have thought we were a bunch of nutters.

The music got louder, mum was the centre of the attention and she loved every minute of it. "Dance, you English children," she'd say, as she knew we would always say we were English, not Portuguese. Everyone was drinking and dancing. I had to secretly admit I enjoyed it too.

Dad took us home much later. Mum slept all the next day, saying it must have been something she had eaten, and she had a bad head. Mum, I think that's what you call a hangover!

Chapter Eighteen

Up to now I haven't mentioned my school days. At first I went to Halkett Place School. I loved school even though we had to wear a school uniform from the age of three. This consisted of a navy blue blazer, a white crisp blue shirt, red tie, navy skirt, white knee-length socks and black shoes. For once we were dressed the same as everyone else – at school at least.

Mum always watched Top of the Pops and would copy the creations the hip singers wore. This might have been cool for a place like London, but Jersey fashion sense was still way behind the times and we hated to look different!

Each morning dad dropped us (my sisters and I) at Scared Car`e. This was a morning club run

Meet Me by the Monkey Bars

by nuns, to take children to school whilst their parents worked. We had to mind our manners and never speak unless spoken to. We always had to walk in two's in a long neat line, and if we spoke whilst walking to school a long ruler would hit us hard on the head. This happened several times to me because I always found it hard to be quiet. However I still liked the nuns.

When we were collected from school they allowed all the children to play Rounders. I think this was their only time to have their freedom because many times I still see the nuns hitching up their long black gowns and running fast to first base. After school was always such a happy time and the nuns would provide cool orange drinks and paste sandwiches and chat away to all the children. I once asked why they couldn't be like this in the mornings. "Good manners and good appearance is everything!" they said.

Infants and Junior school was fun. Other kids thought I was mad when I told them I loved school. Well it beats doing the house-work, I thought.

There was great excitement one day at school. All the children were brought into the hall, we were told we would be doing various experiments to test our senses. Each time an experiment was set up, a teacher called for volunteers. I would wave my hand madly, but I didn't get picked.

Helena Denton

Everyone laughed when Mary had to put her hand in large boxes and guess the item she was touching; she screamed when her hand went in slimy custard. Next Melissa and Anna were picked, ah now I wouldn't hear the last of this. Anna would go on and on how she was picked and I wasn't. Their experiment was to listen to sounds and guess what they were, such as a Hoover or a pin dropping, that sort of thing.

It came to the last experiment, sense of smell. I jumped up before anyone could say anything shouting, "Pick Me!" At last I was picked. I came on stage and felt very important, everyone cheered. I sat on a chair next to a table which had four different foods. I had to smell each one and tell the teacher which was the strongest. There were garlic dishes, curry dishes, sour milk and a large lump of smelly cheese. After smelling each one I just said "No."

Now all the teachers were holding their noses and some children were being taken out of the hall because the smell was so bad. "Well Helena, which is the strongest smell?" the teacher asked. "None, they're all the same." I replied. The teacher told me to stop messing about, but she nearly fell off her chair when I told her, "Well ever since I got a piece of Lego stuck up my nose and went to the hospital I can't smell hardly anything." "Well Helena you never fail to amaze me," she said. I took this as a great compliment and walked off the stage with a

Meet Me by the Monkey Bars

great smile. I looked at Anna's furious face. I had managed to upstage her yet again! Yippee!

Each term a nurse would come to the school and check everyone's hair. She was known as Nitty Nora; I didn't know why I just thought that it was her name. I was always disappointed, as I never got a pink card for the special treatment she told several children they needed to have. However one term Nitty Nora was checking my hair and handed me a pink card telling me to tell my mum that I needed the special treatment.

I couldn't wait to get home, I held this pink card very proudly throughout the day. When I got home I handed the card to my mum; by now mum had developed good English reading but she struggled over the words "head lice". She asked Sue to explain. Suddenly Sue started to scream, "Get her away from me!" I looked at her, had I the plague or something? Now I was frightened.

Sue told her to take me to the bathroom and check my hair. Mum held me over the sink and started to scrape my hair; this was not done lightly and it was very painful. Then to my horror black little creatures filled the sink. I started to scream. I thought they were coming from the tap until mum told me they were coming out of my hair. Mum held me over the sink for over half an hour. I cried, "No, stop!" The worst was to come when dad came home. He was sent to get my "special treatment" as Sue had refused to go saying, "They will think it's in my hair, no way I am getting it." Even when mum threatened to hit her with the slipper she would not budge.

When dad brought the lotion home it was put on my head and a towel was wrapped around my head for over half an hour. It stank terribly and I cried again when I had to have my hair scraped. Mum tried to make me feel better saying no one would know about the head lice. This made me cry more as I remember walking around holding the pink card around the school. Oh the shame.

As we got older mum allowed us to catch the school bus on our own. Each morning she would wake us up and say our breakfasts were on the table then she would go to work, leaving us to get ready for school. I would always go back to bed for an extra ten minutes (even now if I can have those extra lovely minutes in bed I will!) Then I would jump out of bed get ready like a lunatic, grab my school bag in one hand and a slice of cold toast in the other. I then slid down the banisters; this saved vital seconds of time. I would rush outside and run to the bus stop where Sue and Sheila would be waiting with all our friends.

Sometimes they would be on the local bus already, where the bus driver and all the children on the bus would hang out of the windows screaming for me to hurry up. I would run like the wind and a big cheer went up when I reached the bus. Harry the driver would always say, "You'll miss the bus

Meet Me by the Monkey Bars

one of these days, and where will you be then?" No matter how late I was, Harry seemed to work miracles, and we were never late for school. Good Old Harry! However Sue always nudged me and said "Show off, if you got up like us two we wouldn't have to wait for you." Who cares? I thought. I'm here aren't I?

My next school was St Helier Girls School. It was just as nice as my old school. I loved English lessons but hated Maths with a passion. We had to sit in rows. I sat next to a lovely girl called Karen Smith; she had beautiful blonde curly hair and was always smiling. I took a liking to her straight away. Unlike the other Karen in the class, who always would be spiteful to me, "Don't like your hair, cheesy cheesy Portuguese," she would say. This went on for weeks; she had taken a huge dislike to me, boy did she show it. School would have been perfect if it wasn't for her!

However one day I couldn't stand it any longer, she came up to me with a friend (she was never alone) and started being her typical spiteful self. Something snapped in me; instead of walking away I punched her on the nose. I had great delight when she ran around the classroom shouting "She's broken my nose!" Of course I hadn't broken her nose, it was just a nosebleed.

Mrs Lamb frog-marched me to the headmistress, who shook her head with great dismay. "Miss Maria Helena Costa..." (She was the only person

Helena Denton

who addressed me by my full title, not even my mum did!) She gave me a stern lecture on how violence would not be tolerated and that I should behave like a lady at all times. Lucky for me it was a good school, I was never physically punished, in fact nor was anyone else. Unlike the boys' school down the road which always had terrible stories of horrible punishments. When I heard about them it made me pleased to be a girl.

However the Headmistress did punish me. I had to do extra Double Maths! This was the one and only time I cried throughout my school years. It taught me a strong lesson, as I never hit anyone again. What could be worse than extra Double Maths! ....Nothing!

When I got home that day I was expecting mum to get the slipper out for my punishment, but mum and dad just laughed and said the girl got what was coming to her. Dad said he was really insulted over her calling me "Cheesy, cheesy, Portuguese," how dare she? My dad was really cross and he said he would go and complain. I smiled because I knew this wouldn't happen, he hadn't ever stepped inside the school. I thought mum and dad were really strange over this episode; it hadn't bothered them that I had hurt Karen. However they would be very annoyed if I hadn't made my bed. I came to the conclusion my parents were just weird.

Although I loved English lessons the teacher would always complain about how untidy my writing was:

"It's not liked your sister Susan's." I would hear this right through my school years. One lesson Mrs Lamb made me sit next to a girl called Linda. I had to sit and watch her write because she could write "beautifully." I don't know if she thought my handwriting was supposed to change magically, but it never did.

Although Mrs Lamb would constantly moan about the state of my handwriting I always received top marks in any written work I handed in. Mrs Lamb would always write on my essays: "Good content, however your messy writing lets you down".

Mrs Lamb would love the fact I was constantly asking for books to read. I would read any book within a couple of days and Mrs. Lamb would supply as many as I wanted. The other children thought I was bonkers, why would I want to read when I didn't have to? They couldn't understand my pleasure in books.

I always loved Parents' Evening at school, not because of the reason you're thinking; it was because my parents could never attend because of the awkward hours they worked. I would always smile when my maths teacher would say, "Helena your parents will find out about your missing homework on Parents' Evening." Don't hold your breath, I thought. One Parents' Evening, Mrs Lamb told everyone to tidy their desks and put all exercise books in neat piles so they would be easy accessible. Fat chance, I'm not doing that. Waste of time, I thought.

Helena Denton

When I got home that night mum and Sue had their coats on – you guessed it, they were going to attend a Parents' Evening –for the first time since I had started school. Well mum was horrified that all my books had been thrown into the desk, without a care in the world! First she picked up my maths exercise book, which was covered in doodles from the boring maths lessons. In the end I never got to hear what any of the teachers said about me, all mum would say was, "Oh the embarrassment, your desk was so untidy." I thought, if that's all she's got to worry about it, couldn't have been that bad, so who cares?

Our school had regular trips, some to France, London or even to local beauty spots in Jersey, such as camping at Gorey Castle; these all seemed very exciting but for some reason my parents wouldn't allow us to go. I was always very disappointed and felt I was missing out on a great adventure.

I remember sitting in a half empty classroom, with about a dozen other children from the whole school, that for one reason or another could not go on this yearly trip. I was told to sit next to a Spanish girl called Yolanda who could not speak a word of English. The teacher thought because my parents were Portuguese I would be able to understand her. Although I could understand her I wouldn't say a word. Because I had never spoken Portuguese at home there was no way on God's Earth I was going to do it at school. We just smiled at each other. What a long day it was going to be.

Meet Me by the Monkey Bars

After school a group of us sat in the laundrette at the top of our estate and talked about these trips. A lady was doing her washing – Carol's mum. Carol was a very shy girl, a bit of a mystery; no one knew anything about her. Whilst we were talking Carol's mum asked us about these school trips. I didn't want to admit I had never been on a trip so I boasted about how great these trips were.

The next thing I heard Carol was allowed to go on one of the trips. She was going to Elizabeth Castle, a fort which was cut off by the tide a several times a day. This was a great adventure for anyone who ever went there, lucky Carol, she would have great fun, well so they tell me.

A couple of days later I bumped into Carol's mum and asked her if Carol had a good time. Her mum told me on the first night Carol had slipped on the rocks and dislocated her hip and had to be airlifted to hospital. I felt truly guilty because I had been the one to persuade her mum to let her go. Me and my big mouth eh?

I thought that I had a great school life. When I got home and finished my chores, I was free to play with all my friends, doing all the lovely exciting things in Troy Court. What else could a kid want? Life was perfect and I didn't want it to change; but I was in for the biggest shock of my life!

Chapter Nineteen

When I was 12 years old dad told us three girls that we were moving to Gateshead, in north east England. I looked at a map to find out where this place was. It was past London; in fact it was nearly at the top of the map. Dad told us that his friend had offered him a job and he decided that we were to move there. Somewhere new he said. That was that! He was moving the whole family and no matter how much we cried the decision was made, even mum couldn't get him to change his mind.

The day I left Jersey I thought I would never smile again. However that's another story.

Chapter Twenty

Many years later I was married to a wonderful man named John, and had two children: Craig and Natalie. My life was happy but I never forgot my roots. I would often tell my children all about Troy Court.

In 2005 I finally went back to Jersey with my family, in search of Troy Court. We had been in Jersey for about two days and had gone on a trip to the Jersey Zoo. This was a delightful way to spend time in a beautiful environment, which was created by Gerald Durrell, a naturalist who saved endangered animals. The zoo had been one in of those family photos, where the family would be posing for the camera outside the gates but we never got to go inside.

Helena Denton

There was great excitement at the zoo, a baby gorilla had been born on the day we choose to visit. This was proving to be very special day.

On the way home the bus took a different route. I was looking at the beautiful scenery and suddenly shouted, "Stop!" The bus driver slammed on the brakes, as he thought it was an emergency – well it was to me. "This is where I used to live as a child," I rambled on. "Look it's my beloved Troy Court."

Just as we were getting off the bus the driver stared at me and said, "Hey, you're that kid with the two sisters. You always kept my bus waiting. And you're still causing trouble now." I stared back at him. Oh my God, it's Harry, I thought to myself. I couldn't believe it. What a day it was turning out to be.

I was flushed with excitement. John and the children followed me off the bus. "This is the hill where I rode Maurice's bike. Look that's where I spent the five pounds with Anna," I said, pointing to the shop.

I passed several flats until I came to my block. I stroked the pebble dash and looked at the numbers. "Look, sixty-four. That was ours." It didn't seem real. "Look, dad's garage, number four." I was rambling very excitedly, and smiling as the memories came flooding back.

Craig and Natalie were keen to see the famous monkey bars. They were very disappointed that

Meet Me by the Monkey Bars

it was only a small barrier to keep the children off the road. As I turned to my husband John to tell him I was disappointed that they weren't the great monkey bars I had in my mind, suddenly two little girls walked past. "See you later," said one girl. "Yes by the monkey bars," the other replied. And then I was the little girl myself, all those years ago. "Meet you by the monkey bars," I said. It brought tears to my eyes.

Printed in the United Kingdom
by Lightning Source UK Ltd.
124281UK00001B/49-57/A